A Chequered
LEGACY

NICK FAWCETT

The Good, the Bad and the Ugly
of the Church

Book 2: A Lent Course
The Bad and the Ugly

www.kevinmayhew.com

 KM PUBLISHING

First published in Great Britain in 2014 by Kevin Mayhew Ltd
Buxhall, Stowmarket, Suffolk IP14 3BW
Tel: +44 (0) 1449 737978 Fax: +44 (0) 1449 737834
E-mail: info@kevinmayhew.com

www.kevinmayhew.com

ISBN 978 1 84867 730 2
Catalogue No. 1501452

Cover design by Rob Mortonson
© Images used under licence from Shutterstock Inc.
Typeset by Richard Weaver

Printed and bound in Great Britain

Contents

About the author

Brought up in Southend-in-Sea, Essex, Nick Fawcett trained for the Baptist ministry at Bristol and Oxford, before serving churches in Lancashire and Cheltenham. He subsequently spent three years as a chaplain with the Christian movement Toc H, before focusing on writing and editing, which he continues with today, despite wrestling with myeloma, a currently incurable cancer of the bone marrow. He lives with his wife, Deborah, and two children – Samuel and Kate – in Wellington, Somerset, worshipping, when able, at the local Anglican church. A keen walker, he delights in the beauty of the Somerset and Devon countryside around his home, his numerous books owing much to the inspiration he unfailingly finds there.

Introduction

What is the greatest enemy of the Christian faith? Strange as it may seem, the answer could, with some justification, be put forward as the Church. Such a suggestion sounds ludicrous, doesn't it – a contradiction in terms! And so, to a point, it *is*, for beyond doubt the Church is also the greatest friend that the Christian faith will ever have. Yet, as many a militant atheist, or even sceptical agnostic, will quickly point out, the Church's history is hardly one to be proud of, littered as it is with all kinds of errors, aberrations, even crimes that make a mockery of everything Jesus taught and that Christians are meant to stand for. The Spanish Inquisition, burning of witches, wars in the name of religion, persecution of other Christians or those of other faiths, and, more recently, rampant sexism and homophobia, not to mention child abuse scandals, have repeatedly dragged the Church's name through the mud; truly a legacy to be ashamed of. Sadly, yet seemingly almost inevitably, organised religion by definition runs the risk of destroying the very thing it sets out to embody and safeguard. The kernel of truth that gives it birth becomes lost under a husk of accretions, as well-meaning (and not-so-well-meaning) believers seek to prescribe just what that truth is. Each defines God in their own image and, usually, according to their own interests.

Yet, as I've said, such a negative and bleak assessment does not give the complete picture. In all kinds of ways the Church has been a force for good across the centuries, seeking to make known the love of Christ in word and deed, striving in ways large and small to help build a better world. I've been privileged personally to know a host of wonderful Christians who throughout their lives have attempted to translate faith into action, their example offering untold inspiration and enrichment. And a significant percentage of voluntary caring work within this country is still undertaken by Christian believers and organisations, seeking to ameliorate the lot of others, to the extent that if their services were to be withdrawn, the consequences for many, and for society at large, would be devastating. For all its unquestionable faults, the Church also has numerous virtues to learn from and build upon.

In this two-volume study book I explore what – to steal the title of the classic spaghetti western – we might term the good, the bad and the ugly of the Church. The Advent booklet looks at the positive, celebrating some of the achievements of Christian believers across the years in terms of building a better world, and asking what their efforts and example might teach us today. In this Lent book, we focus on some of the faults of the Church; faults that call us to reflect, confess, repent and work as best we can for a better, more enlightened future. Let me urge you to treat both books as a pair, and not to use one without moving on to the other. To do the latter would risk giving you a completely false picture, either reinforcing a misplaced sense of complacency or leading to an overly jaundiced appraisal of the Church, past, present and future. We have a chequered history, there's no getting away from it: a mixture of the inspiring and appalling, wonderful and awful, and we need to learn from both. Through doing so honestly, we may perhaps open the way for God to help us become more fully the people he would have us be.

Nick Fawcett

I'm right, you're wrong: the blight of religious intolerance

Opening prayer

Almighty God,
so many within our world seek to know and serve you better,
yet that very seeking and knowing seems so often to divide
and estrange
rather than draw people together,
alienating us from you
and from one another.
Open our hearts to traditions other than our own,
and to all that they might teach us
Open our minds to people who think differently from us,
and to insights they might share.
Save us from automatically assuming we are right about everything,
that we have grasped the truth,
the whole truth
and nothing but the truth,
and, above all,
save us from hostility towards those who disagree with us
or whose understanding of you does not correspond to our own.
Teach us to stay true to our convictions,
but to treat others also with respect,
always being open to you speaking in ways
and through people,
that we least expect.
Amen.

Key passage

'I ask not only on behalf of these, but also on behalf of those who will believe in me through their word, that they may all be one. As you, Father, are in me and I am in you, may they also be in us, so that the world may believe that you have sent me.'

John 17:20, 21

Ice-breaker

Invite participants to pair off and play a game of draughts together (you will need to prepare for this before the session, ensuring you have sufficient sets of draughts and boards to accommodate everyone). Set a time limit to ensure that this ice-breaker does not take over the session.

Introduction

Of all the accusations levelled against religion, perhaps the most common is that it has persistently led to division, hatred, persecution and even war. The charge is hard to argue against, for history is indeed littered with examples of such evils, not least the history of Christianity. It started off, ironically, with the boot on the other foot, Christians being the persecuted minority in a hostile and suspicious world, but once the Emperor Constantine made Christianity the official religion of the Roman Empire, the situation very swiftly changed. Before long it was Christians doing the persecuting, and they took to it in a big way. 'Heretics' – namely, those whose views differed from those in authority – were tortured and burnt at the stake; pagan religions were ruthlessly suppressed, their followers forced to convert on pain of punishment or death; Muslims were attacked in the Holy Land during a series of Crusades, many of these ending in massacres on both sides; Jews were increasingly victimised, forced to the margins of society or into exile; 'witches' were hunted down and, after farcical trials, executed; and so we could continue. The slaughter of Protestants and Catholics during the Tudor and Stuart years in England has gone down in our history as one of the most notorious examples of religious persecution, as has the religious divide in Northern Ireland and the so-called Troubles there, The very fact that various denominations continue to exist – Roman Catholic, Anglican, Baptist, Methodist, and so forth – despite years of ecumenical dialogue, and that no love seems to be lost sometimes between Christians of various persuasions, is seen by many as evidence of the inherently divisive nature of religion. And all this is barely to touch on Christianity's relations with other faiths, particularly Islam, Christian–Muslim tensions having led to unspeakable horrors being perpetrated in Bosnia, Armenia, Africa and numerous other parts of the world.

So where does this leave us? Is Christianity, by definition, divisive? Does our faith add to this world's troubles rather than help to ameliorate them? Is all our talk of peace and reconciliation, love and respect for others, merely a cover disguising the less palatable reality of what we stand for? To be fair to Christianity, many of its worst excesses in terms of violent persecution have come about when religion has become entwined with sectarian politics – always a noxious combination – but that cannot be used to let us off the hook. Let's pause for a moment and see what the Bible has to say concerning our relations with others, particularly those of other faiths or different persuasions.

Bible verses

The Bible, on this issue as in so many, offers us mixed messages. There's no getting away from the fact that several Old Testament passages not only encourage slaughter and genocide but present this as God's express command (e.g. Deuteronomy 2:34; 3:6; 7:2; 13:15; 20:16, 17; Joshua 6:21; Joshua 10:40; 1 Samuel 15:2, 3). We need to wrestle with such verses and come up with some kind of explanation for them that holds water; one that can somehow reconcile a God of hatred and violence with the One we claim to be all good and all loving. Can any literal and fundamentalist approach to Scripture ever truly bring together these two poles, or do we have to accept that much of what we find in the Old

11

Testament represents a fundamentally flawed understanding of God that needs to be corrected by the picture offered by Jesus in the New Testament, with its emphasis on love and forgiveness? What do you think?

Other passages in the Bible can be taken in two ways, on the one hand seeming to oppose division yet on the other offering ammunition to those who might seek to divide themselves from others, with all the attendant consequences.

Romans 16:17

I urge you, brothers and sisters, to keep an eye on those who cause dissensions and offences, in opposition to the teaching that you have learned; avoid them.

1 Corinthians 7:13-16

And if any woman has a husband who is an unbeliever, and he consents to live with her, she should not divorce him. For the unbelieving husband is made holy through his wife, and the unbelieving wife is made holy through her husband. Otherwise, your children would be unclean, but as it is, they are holy. But if the unbelieving partner separates, let it be so; in such a case the brother or sister is not bound. It is to peace that God has called you. Wife, for all you know, you might save your husband. Husband, for all you know, you might save your wife.

Titus 3:10, 11

After a first and second admonition, have nothing more to do with anyone who causes divisions, since you know that such a person is perverted and sinful, being self-condemned.

2 John 1:10, 11

Do not receive into the house or welcome anyone who comes to you and does not bring this teaching; for to welcome is to participate in the evil deeds of such a person.

Jude vv. 2-4

Beloved, while eagerly preparing to write to you about the salvation we share, I find it necessary to write and appeal to you to contend for the faith that was once for all entrusted to the saints. For certain intruders have stolen in among you, people who long ago were designated for this condemnation as ungodly, who pervert the grace of our God into licentiousness and deny our only Master and Lord, Jesus Christ.

Other passages, again, emphasise the importance of unity. Read and reflect upon the following, and look again at the key verses from John 21 given at the start of this session, in which Jesus expresses his longing for the unity of all his people:

Psalms 133:1

How very good and pleasant it is when kindred live together in unity!

Matthew 7:12

'In everything do to others as you would have them do to you; for this is the law and the prophets.'

Mark 9:40

'Whoever is not against us is for us.'

Luke 9:50

But Jesus said to him, 'Do not stop him; for whoever is not against you is for you.'

1 Corinthians 1:10

Now I appeal to you, brothers and sisters, by the name of our Lord Jesus Christ, that all of you should be in agreement and that there should be no divisions among you, but that you should be united in the same mind and the same purpose.

Ephesians 4:1-3

I therefore, the prisoner in the Lord, beg you to lead a life worthy of the calling to which you have been called, with all humility and gentleness, with patience, bearing with one another in love, making every effort to maintain the unity of the Spirit in the bond of peace.

Ephesians 4:30-32

And do not grieve the Holy Spirit of God, with which you were marked with a seal for the day of redemption. Put away from you all bitterness and wrath and anger and wrangling and slander, together with all malice, and be kind to one another, tender-hearted, forgiving one another, as God in Christ has forgiven you.

Philippians 4:5

Let your gentleness be known to everyone. The Lord is near.

1 Peter 3:8-11

Finally, all of you, have unity of spirit, sympathy, love for one another, a tender heart, and a humble mind. Do not repay evil for evil or abuse for abuse; but, on the contrary, repay with a blessing. It is for this that you were called – that you might inherit a blessing. For 'Those who desire life and desire to see good days, let them keep their tongues from evil and their lips from speaking deceit; let them turn away from evil and do good; let them seek peace and pursue it.'

Study

What do the verses above tell us about the way we should live in relation to other Christians and people of other faiths? The exhortation to love and forgive others is all very well, but what does it mean in practice? How should we act when we disagree with people over important aspects of belief or over the very nature of faith itself? In Mark and Luke, Jesus appears to indicate we should be as open as possible to those who see things differently to us ('Whoever is not against us is for us'), but in the Gospel of Matthew (12:30) he seemingly suggests the opposite: 'Whoever is not with me is against me, and whoever does not gather with me scatters.' It's hard to pinpoint an unequivocal message. Yet doesn't that take us to the heart of the matter? Scripture can be used to support all kinds of beliefs and doctrines. For centuries Christians have disagreed on all kinds of issues, and they probably always will. On countless matters, we cannot prove that we're right, much though we may believe that we are. What matters is how we deal with that; whether we're able to agree to disagree, and to disagree in love. Yes, we need to stay true to our convictions, whether we're talking to a Christian of another persuasion or a person of another faith, but we also need to listen to and respect their views, being open to potential truths in what they're saying and to the possibility that we may need to revise our own beliefs accordingly.

The ecumenical movement has long pioneered such an approach, and though, sadly, it has its detractors, its efforts have seen massive strides in terms of fostering good relations between Christians. Organic unity remains an elusive – and perhaps unrealistic (even undesirable?) – goal, but Christians of most established denominations share and work together as perhaps never before, much that previously divided them no longer being seen as obstacles to cooperation.

More controversial for some is interfaith dialogue. Opponents of this accuse its proponents of aiming to water down the gospel, reducing the Christian faith to an amorphous amalgam of different ideas drawn from various world religions. But that is far from the intended aim, which, rather, is simply to foster genuine discussion and understanding. Once again, this will frequently involve agreeing to disagree, but at its best such dialogue can help to break down barriers of prejudice and misconception and lead to genuine cooperation despite very real differences.

Notwithstanding what some may say, it is not *religious differences* that we need to avoid, but *religious intolerance*. Differences are inevitable and intrinsically healthy, provided that we are willing to listen to and learn from one others, seeing those differences as an opportunity rather than threat. None of us has the whole truth, however much we may think otherwise. We need the insights of others to help challenge and stretch our own beliefs. It's when we're utterly convinced of our rightness – intolerant of all other opinions, and of the people who hold them – that division ensues. History has shown all too clearly where that can lead.

Discussion

- Is it possible to have firm convictions yet to respect the convictions of others? What prevents us from doing so? Does dialogue inevitably involve watering down one's own convictions?
- In what aspects of life and faith are Christians still intolerant of others? What causes such intolerance? What attitudes and actions tend to characterise it?
- Clearly there are some areas in which Christians (and people in general) need to be intolerant; for example, of injustice, of intolerance itself, of the sort of wrongs discussed in this book, etc. Is there a danger of tolerance going too far? How do we avoid that?
- How would you answer someone who claims that religion, and Christianity specifically, has been responsible for many of the most polarising divisions in human history, and that it is still a major cause of division between people today?
- Should the Church aim for organic unity (no denominations)? Provided that Christians truly respect and work with one another, are differences between them a sign of health? Are there divisions in the Church not covered or touched by ecumenical dialogue? If so, what are these and can they be overcome?
- What do you think of interfaith dialogue? What do you see as its dangers and possibilities?

Quotes

Reflect individually on the following quotations for a moment, then discuss together which, if any, people found most helpful. What point is each making? What lessons can be learned from them? What challenge do they make to us, personally, and to the Church in general.

- People who prefer to believe the worst of others will breed war and religious persecutions while the world lasts. (Dorothy L. Sayers)
- Anger and intolerance are the enemies of correct understanding. (Mahatma Gandhi)
- Dialogue and education for peace can help free our hearts from the impulse toward intolerance and the rejection of others. (Daisaku Ikeda)
- Cruel persecutions and intolerance are not accidents, but grow out of the very essence of religion, namely, its absolute claims. (Morris Raphael Cohen)
- Religious wars are not caused by the fact that there is more than one religion, but by the spirit of intolerance . . . the spread of which can only be regarded as the total eclipse of human reason. (Montesquieu)
- Christian creeds and doctrines, the clergy's own fatal inventions, through all the ages has made of Christendom a slaughterhouse, and divided it into sects of inextinguishable hatred for one another. (Thomas Jefferson)
- The need of the moment is not one religion, but mutual respect and tolerance of the devotees of the different religions. (Mahatma Gandhi)
- Christians, needless to say, utterly detest one another; they slander each other constantly with the vilest forms of abuse, and cannot come to any sort of agreement in their teaching. Each sect brands its own, fills the head of its own with deceitful nonsense. (Celsus)
- Wide differences of opinion in matters of religious, political, and social belief must exist if conscience and intellect alike are not to be stunted, if there is to be room for healthy growth. (Theodore Roosevelt)
- I very much dislike the intolerance and moralism of many Christians, and feel more sympathy with Honest Doubters than with them. (A. N. Wilson)

- Discord is the great ill of mankind; and tolerance is the only remedy for it. (Voltaire)
- No human trait deserves less tolerance in everyday life, and gets less, than intolerance. (Giacomo Leopardi)
- In order to have faith in his own path, he does not need to prove that someone else's path is wrong. (Paulo Coelho)
- Intolerance betrays want of faith in one's cause. (Mahatma Gandhi)
- To know a person's religion we need not listen to his profession of faith but must find his brand of intolerance. (Eric Hoffer)
- If people but knew their own religion, how tolerant they would become, and how free from any grudge against the religion of others. (Hazrat Inayat Khan)
- Bigotry and intolerance, silenced by argument, endeavours to silence by persecution, in old days by fire and sword, in modern days by the tongue. (Charles Simmons)
- We must learn to live together as brothers or perish together as fools. (Martin Luther King Jr)
- Tolerance of intolerance is cowardice. (Ayaan Hirsi Ali)
- I'm a writer of faith who worries about the intolerance of religion. I look at the past and fear we haven't learned from it. I believe that humanity is capable of evil as well as great acts of courage and goodness. I have hope. Deep down, I believe in the human spirit, although sometimes that belief is shaken. (Julianna Baggott)
- If I do not believe as you believe, it proves that you do not believe as I believe, and that is all that it proves. (Thomas Paine)
- If we cannot end now our differences, at least we can help make the world safe for diversity. (John F. Kennedy)
- I never will, by any word or act, bow to the shrine of intolerance or admit a right of inquiry into the religious opinions of others. (Thomas Jefferson)
- Don't get so tolerant that you tolerate intolerance. (Bill Maher)
- True tolerance is loving your enemy, accepting their differences and remaining humble. (Denise Stark)

- You can safely assume that you've created God in your own image when it turns out that God hates all the same people you do. (Anne Lamott)
- People are never so completely and enthusiastically evil as when they act out of religious conviction. (Umberto Eco)
- History is full of religious wars; but, we must take care to observe, it was not the multiplicity of religions that produced these wars, it was the intolerating spirit which animated that one which thought she had the power of governing. (Montesquieu)
- Of all bad men religious bad men are the worst. (C. S. Lewis)
- Intolerance is a species of violence and therefore against our creed. (Mahatma Gandhi)
- If you have two religions in your land, the two will cut each other's throats; but if you have thirty religions, they dwell in peace. (Voltaire)
- Religion divides us, while it is our human characteristics that bind us to each other. (Hermann Bondi)
- Men never do evil so completely and cheerfully as when they do it with religious conviction. (Blaise Pascal)
- We have just enough religion to make us hate, but not enough to make us love one another. (Jonathan Swift)
- Being a Methodist, a Catholic, or a Baptist does not make one a disciple, it only makes him a Methodist, a Catholic, or a Baptist, who may or may not be a daily follower of Jesus Christ. (Michael Phillips)
- The Institutional Church (*ecclesia*) has killed only two kinds of people: Those who do not believe in the teachings of Jesus Christ, and those who do. (Will Durant)
- Organised Christianity has probably done more to retard the ideals that were its founder's than any other agency in the world. (Richard Le Gallienne)
- There is nothing wrong with believing in a God. There is everything wrong in believing in a religion. (Unknown)
- I have carefully examined what it means to be a heretic, and I cannot make it mean more than this: 'A heretic is a man with whom you disagree.' (Sebastian Castellio)

- Difference of opinion is advantageous in religion. The several sects perform the office of a *Censor morum* over each other. Is uniformity attainable? Millions of innocent men, women, and children, since the introduction of Christianity, have been burnt, tortured, fined, imprisoned; yet we have not advanced one inch towards uniformity. What has been the effect of coercion? To make one half the world fools, and the other half hypocrites. To support roguery and error all over the earth. (Thomas Jefferson)

Final thoughts

Reminded of the involvement of the Church, or Christians, in so many brutal acts of religious intolerance across history, we will most probably feel a sense of shame and a desire to disassociate ourselves from such things. Indeed, we may almost sometimes feel like washing our hands of the Church entirely, rather than have anything to do with such a legacy. Happily, things have moved on considerably since most of the worst incidents in the Church's history, Christians today – at least in this country and most of Western Europe – typically being involved in moves towards peace and reconciliation rather than the opposite. Yet that's not entirely the case. While we are unlikely to see, let alone condone, any acts of religious persecution, intolerance is still all too real, as we will be reminded during the course of this book. Christians still condemn other Christians, question their faith, argue over this or that issue and split one from another. And each of us, in our own small way, can be part of that, seeds of division lurking within us all, just waiting for the opportunity to germinate given the right conditions. Use this Lent not only to ask God's forgiveness for the intolerance and persecution of which the Church has been guilty in the past but also to seek his cleansing from whatever within you might contribute to dividing and destroying in the present.

Closing prayer

Lord Jesus Christ,
you call us to love one another;
forgive the way that Christians across the centuries have
frequently done the opposite,
hating those who think differently than they do,
persecuting those whose interpretation of the Bible clashes with
their own.
You call us to be one;
forgive the fact that, too often,
it has been our divisions rather than unity that has caught the
attention of the world,
speaking not of your grace and goodness
but of human weakness and intolerance.
You call us to make you known;
forgive the way the Church has sometimes forced its faith
upon others,
and in so doing has put across a false picture of who and what
you are.
Forgive the countless evils that have been perpetrated in the
name of religion;
evils that have besmirched your name
and led people away from rather than towards you.
Teach us always to be open to you and to others,
and truly to walk the way of Christ,
so that the world may know we are Christians by the sincerity of
our love.
Amen.

Practising what we preach?
The blight of hypocrisy

Opening prayer

Loving God,
you call us to walk the way of Christ,
to live in such a manner that his light and love shines through us.
We yearn to do that,
but though the spirit is willing, the flesh is weak,
such that the message we put across is often very different from
the one we intend,
speaking more of *us* than of him –
of our faults and weaknesses
prejudices and preconceptions,
judgemental and self-righteous attitudes.
Forgive us,
and challenge us to be more loving,
more caring
and more consistent in all we do,
so that our words and deeds,
practice and preaching,
may speak with one voice:
of *you*.
Amen.

Key passage

But be doers of the word, and not merely hearers who deceive themselves. For if any are hearers of the word and not doers, they are like those who look at themselves in a mirror; for they look at themselves and, on going away, immediately forget what they were like. But those who look into the perfect law, the law of liberty, and persevere, being not hearers who forget but doers who act – they will be blessed in their doing.

James 1:22-25

Ice-breaker

Invite participants to pair off and play a variant game of draughts together – see the site http://www.di.fc.ul.pt/~jpn/gv/checkers.htm for details of variants (e.g. Canadian Checkers, German Checkers, Italian Checkers, Russian Checkers, Spanish Checkers, Thai Checkers, Turkish Checkers etc.) and how to play them. (You will need to prepare for this before the session, ensuring you have sufficient sets of draughts and boards to accommodate everyone. You will also need to succinctly explain the rules of the variation.) Set a time limit to ensure that this ice-breaker does not take over the session.

Introduction

We've all heard it, haven't we? It's probably the most common accusation levelled against Christians: that we're just a bunch of self-righteous hypocrites who say one thing and do another, presuming to judge others when we're far from being whiter than white ourselves. Is that assessment true? Of course it is – to a point anyway. None of us are perfect, far from it; that's precisely why we become part of the Church in the first place: because we recognise how much is wrong in our lives, how flawed and foolish we are, how far we are from being the people God wants us to be. Yet is that the message we put across? Probably not. And there are good reasons for that.

On the one hand, we don't want to come across like Uriah Heep, forever wringing our hands at our own shortcomings. I'm reminded of that wonderful scene in *Monty Python and the Holy Grail* in which King Arthur and his men abjectly abase themselves before God. 'Oh, don't grovel!' God barks impatiently. 'If there's one thing I can't stand, it's people grovelling.' 'Sorry!' says Arthur meekly. 'And don't apologise,' groans God. 'Every time I try to talk to someone it's "sorry this" and "forgive me that" and "I'm not worthy".' In other words, God doesn't like cloying humility, and, understandably, neither does anyone else, so we rightly try to avoid it.

Furthermore, as Christians we genuinely try to live better lives, following what we believe to be God's wishes more closely, and encouraging others to do the same. The impression we can give as a result is that we consider ourselves better than others, more deserving of God's blessing, and, unfortunately, Christians sometimes fall into the trap of believing just that, judging and condemning others as a result. It's a danger we must avoid at all costs, for the fact is we are not in any way better, most of us being all too aware of how far we fall short. Many non-Christians put us to shame by the quality of their lifestyles, the extent of their generosity, the breadth of their compassion and the sincerity of their love. Time and again our deeds fail to measure up to our words, our actions to our good intentions.

Let's pause then, for a moment, and see what the Bible has to tell us concerning the relationship between words and deeds.

Bible verses

The Bible has much to say about hypocrisy, some of its choicest words and most memorable passages being devoted to denouncing it. Chief among these is Matthew 23 (compare also Luke 11:39-52), in which Jesus launches into an extended diatribe against the hypocrisy of the scribes and Pharisees. Read and reflect upon the passages below, discussing any key points that come out of them.

Psalm 101:7

No one who practises deceit shall remain in my house; no one who utters lies shall continue in my presence.

Proverbs 26:23-26

Like the glaze covering an earthen vessel are smooth lips with an evil heart. An enemy dissembles in speaking while harbouring deceit within; when an enemy speaks graciously, do not believe it, for there are seven abominations concealed within; though hatred is covered with guile, the enemy's wickedness will be exposed in the assembly.

Isaiah 1:11-15 (see also Amos 5:21-27)

What to me is the multitude of your sacrifices? says the Lord; I have had enough of burnt-offerings of rams and the fat of fed beasts; I do not delight in the blood of bulls, or of lambs, or of goats. When you come to appear before me, who asked this from your hand? Trample my courts no more; bringing offerings is futile; incense is an abomination to me. New moon and sabbath and calling of convocation – I cannot endure solemn assemblies with iniquity. Your new moons and your appointed festivals my soul hates; they have become a burden to me, I am weary of bearing them. When you stretch out your hands, I will hide my eyes from you; even though you make many prayers, I will not listen; your hands are full of blood.

Isaiah 29:13

. . . these people draw near with their mouths and honour me with their lips, while their hearts are far from me, and their worship of me is a human commandment learned by rote.

Isaiah 58:2-5

Yet day after day they seek me and delight to know my ways, as if they were a nation that practised righteousness and did not forsake the ordinance of their God; they ask of me righteous judgements, they delight to draw near to God. 'Why do we fast, but you do not see? Why humble ourselves, but you do not notice?' Look, you serve your own interest on your fast-day, and oppress all your workers. Look, you fast only to quarrel and to fight and to strike with a wicked fist. Such fasting as you do today will not make your voice heard on high. Is such the fast that I choose, a day to humble oneself? Is it to bow down the head like a bulrush, and to lie in sackcloth and ashes? Will you call this a fast, a day acceptable to the Lord?

Matthew 6:1-5

'Beware of practising your piety before others in order to be seen by them; for then you have no reward from your Father in heaven. So whenever you give alms, do not sound a trumpet before you, as the hypocrites do in the synagogues and in the streets, so that they may be praised by others. Truly I tell you, they have received their reward. But when you give alms, do not let your left hand know what your right hand is doing, so that your alms may be done in secret; and your Father who sees in secret will reward you. And whenever you pray, do not be like the hypocrites; for they love to stand and pray in the synagogues and at the street corners, so that they may be seen by others. Truly I tell you, they have received their reward.'

Matthew 6:16

'And whenever you fast, do not look dismal, like the hypocrites, for they disfigure their faces so as to show others that they are fasting. Truly I tell you, they have received their reward.'

Matthew 7:21-23

'Not everyone who says to me, "Lord, Lord", will enter the kingdom of heaven, but only one who does the will of my Father in heaven. On that day many will say to me, "Lord, Lord, did we not prophesy in your name, and cast out demons in your name, and do many deeds of power in your name?" Then I will declare to them, "I never knew you; go away from me, you evildoers."'

Mark 7:6-8 (see also Matthew 15:7-9)

He said to them, 'Isaiah prophesied rightly about you hypocrites, as it is written, "This people honours me with their lips, but their hearts are far from me; in vain do they worship me, teaching human precepts as doctrines." You abandon the commandment of God and hold to human tradition.'

Luke 6:46

'Why do you call me "Lord, Lord", and do not do what I tell you?'

Luke 13:14-16

But the leader of the synagogue, indignant because Jesus had cured on the sabbath, kept saying to the crowd, 'There are six days on which work ought to be done; come on those days and be cured, and not on the sabbath day.' But the Lord answered him and said, 'You hypocrites! Does not each of you on the sabbath untie his ox or his donkey from the manger, and lead it away to give it water? And ought not this woman, a daughter of Abraham whom Satan bound for eighteen long years, be set free from this bondage on the sabbath day?'

Luke 16:15

So he said to them, 'You are those who justify yourselves in the sight of others; but God knows your hearts; for what is prized by human beings is an abomination in the sight of God.'

Luke 20:46, 47

'Beware of the scribes, who like to walk around in long robes, and love to be greeted with respect in the market-places, and to have the best seats in the synagogues and places of honour at banquets. They devour widows' houses and for the sake of appearance say long prayers. They will receive the greater condemnation.'

James 2:14-17

What good is it, my brothers and sisters, if you say you have faith but do not have works? Can faith save you? If a brother or sister is naked and lacks daily food, and one of you says to them, 'Go in peace; keep warm and eat your fill', and yet you do not supply their bodily needs, what is the good of that? So faith by itself, if it has no works, is dead.

1 John 1:6

If we say that we have fellowship with him while we are walking in darkness, we lie and do not do what is true.

1 John 2:4

Whoever says, 'I have come to know him', but does not obey his commandments, is a liar, and in such a person the truth does not exist.

1 John 2:9

Whoever says, 'I am in the light', while hating a brother or sister, is still in the darkness.

1 John 3:16, 17

We know love by this, that he laid down his life for us – and we ought to lay down our lives for one another. How does God's love abide in anyone who has the world's goods and sees a brother or sister in need and yet refuses help?

1 John 4:20

Those who say, 'I love God', and hate their brothers or sisters, are liars; for those who do not love a brother or sister whom they have seen, cannot love God whom they have not seen.

Study

Child sex abuse among priests, tele-evangelists embezzling funds donated by gullible viewers, clergy conducting adulterous relationships, treasurers running off with church funds or investing them in dubious markets; bishops denouncing vices that they themselves turn out to be guilty of – these are the sort of blatantly hypocritical acts that hit the news headlines and give the Church a bad name, and sadly some of them have turned out to be much more common than we might have anticipated. Yet hypocrisy, as we've already indicated, is not limited to such high-profile cases; it's something each of us can be guilty of and all too often are. We don't mean it to happen, but it does, for as Christians we are constantly trying to live up to high ideals that ultimately are beyond us. Do any of us, for example, truly love our enemies, turn the other cheek, give to whoever begs from us, put the interests of others before our own, and so forth? We may possibly manage to do so on occasions, but time and again we will much more likely fail.

To avoid the charge of hypocrisy, we need to do three things. First we must honest and up front about how hard we find it to live up to our convictions, not in an overly pious or negative way, but making it plain that we are all too aware of the gulf between what we want to do and what we actually succeed in doing. We need to make it clear that we make no claim to be perfect or even good. Rather, we are those who have a vision of what life could be and who want to bring that to fulfilment, even though we find it a constant struggle to do so. To put it in biblical language, we are not saints looking down on others, but sinners inviting them to share with us in striving to build a better world.

Second, we need to avoid passing judgement. Christians are frequently swift to condemn what they see as the moral vices of society, particularly in matters relating to sex, which the Church has always been particularly hung up about. We forget the truth of that saying 'There but for the grace of God go I', and we forget also the often-repeated biblical injunction not to judge others lest we be judged ourselves. Of course some things are wrong, and we should strive to avoid them. Of course we would not encourage them in others either, but in all our dealings we need to approach people in a spirit of love, forgiveness and understanding rather than of sanctimonious censure.

Finally, even though we know we can never achieve it solely through our own efforts, we need to try harder to be the people God wants us to be, to live in such a way that our words and actions tally more consistently. Our prayer needs to be along the lines of the wonderful hymn of John Hunter's, written in 1889:

Dear Master, in whose life I see
all that I would, but fail to be,
let Thy clear light forever shine,
to shame and guide this life of mine.

Though what I dream and what I do
in my weak days are always two,
help me, oppressed by things undone,
O Thou whose deeds and dreams were one!

We'll never fully achieve that, probably never even come near it, but the more closely our aims measure up to reality, the more seriously people will take us, and the less open we'll be to the charge of hypocrisy that has turned so many off the Church.

Discussion

• How would you define hypocrisy?
• In what areas of discipleship are you guilty of saying one thing and doing another? What aspects of Christian commitment do you find hardest to live up to? Is it ever possible to avoid the charge of hypocrisy completely?
• Which of the Bible passages above spoke most powerfully to you? Which did you find most challenging?
• In what ways has the Church in times past been most guilty of hypocrisy? In what areas of life could the charge be levelled against Christians today? Have non-Christian friends of yours made the accusation?
• Is it possible for the Church to be non-judgemental yet still to stand up for its convictions and make a moral stand in the world? How can it go about this?
• What steps could you take today to eliminate at least some of the possible charges of hypocrisy against you?

Quotes

Reflect individually on the following quotations for a moment, then discuss together which, if any, people found most helpful. What point is each making? What lessons can be learned from them? What challenge do they make to us, personally, and to the Church in general.

• Hypocrisy can afford to be magnificent in its promises, for never intending to go beyond promise, it costs nothing. (Edmund Burke)

- Go put your creed into your deed. (Ralph Waldo Emerson)
- He does not believe that does not live according to his belief. (Sigmund Freud)
- I am surrounded by priests who repeat incessantly that their kingdom is not of this world, and yet they lay their hands on everything they can get. (Napoleon Bonaparte)
- An immoral character, glossed with religious pretention, is like a rotten egg with an Easter colouring. (Lewis F. Korns)
- They are not all saints who use holy water. (English proverb)
- In nothing do the words of Christian liturgy strike the ears of contemporary men and women as 'empty ritual' so much as when they speak of a loving, Spirit-filled community where none is visible. (Leonel Mitchell)
- I do not find in orthodox Christianity one redeeming feature. (Thomas Jefferson)
- The Christian resolution to find the world ugly and bad has made the world ugly and bad. (Friedrich Nietzsche)
- The human race in the course of time has taken the liberty of softening and softening Christianity until at last we have contrived to make it exactly the opposite of what it is in the New Testament. (Søren Kierkegaard)
- Hypocrisy is the homage vice pays to virtue. (François de La Rochefoucauld)
- If Satan ever laughs, it must be at hypocrites; they are the greatest dupes he has; they serve him better than any others, and receive no wages. (Charles Caleb Colton)
- I care not for a man's religion whose dog and cat are not the better for it. (Abraham Lincoln)
- Why do born-again people so often make you wish they'd never been born the first time? (Katherine Whitehorn)
- If it weren't for Christians, I'd be a Christian. (Mahatma Gandhi)
- I might believe in the Redeemer if His followers looked more Redeemed. (Fredrick Nietzsche)
- It has always seemed unfair to me that many churches (and some individual Christians) keep careful records on how many converts they make to Christianity, but never keep any record of how many they drive away from Christ! (Ray C. Stedman)

- The people who make wars, the people who reduce their fellows to slavery, the people who kill and torture and tell lies in the name of their sacred causes, the really evil people in a word – these are never the publicans and the sinners. No, they're the virtuous, respectable men, who have the finest feelings, the best brains, the noblest ideals. (Aldous Huxley)
- The Church is always trying to get other people to reform; it might not be a bad idea to reform itself a little by way of example. (Mark Twain)
- Religion is the fashionable substitute for belief. (Oscar Wilde)
- The true hypocrite is the one who ceases to perceive his deception, the one who lies with sincerity. (André Gide)
- The best argument for Christianity is Christians: their joy, their certainty, their completeness. But the strongest argument against Christianity is also Christians – when they are sombre and joyless, when they are self-righteous and smug in complacent consecration, when they are narrow and repressive, then Christianity dies a thousand deaths. (Joe Aldrich)
- Everyday, people are straying away from the Church and going back to God. (Lennie Bruce)
- It does not follow that a man is a hypocrite because his actions give the lie to his words. If he at one time seems a saint, and at other times a sinner, he possibly is both in reality, as well as in appearance. A person may be fond of vice and of virtue too; and practise one or the other, according to the temptation of the moment. (William Hazlitt)
- Sincerity makes the very least person to be of more value than the most talented hypocrite. (Charles Spurgeon)
- I would rather spend every Sunday of my life hanging off a cliff to rescue someone than spend one more time sitting in a pew next to hypocrites that talk about what they will do to better themselves and the world when they get around to it. (Shannon L. Alder)
- Let your religion be less of a theory and more of a love affair. (G.K. Chesterton)

Final thoughts

'Do as I say, not as I do,' we may sometimes urge others, but in our heart we know that's wasted advice, for it's very much the case that actions speak louder than words. We may espouse the loftiest ideals in the world, but if we show no indication of wanting to live up to them then people will understandably be sceptical of our commitment. It's no coincidence that those who most commonly catch the public imagination are those whose words and deeds are consistent: people like Mahatma Gandhi, Mother Theresa, Martin Luther King and Nelson Mandela. Live in such a way that we put our money where our mouth is and people may well sit up and start to take notice of our life and witness; do the opposite and we can be quite certain that they will do the opposite too, our claims – however fine or well intentioned – leaving them cold.

Closing prayer

Father God,
forgive us,
for too often we have said one thing and done another.
We have spoken of loving others,
but have had thoughts only for ourselves;
of forgiving,
but have nursed grievances;
of walking your way,
but have walked our own way instead.
Time and again our good intentions have proved hollow,
the claims we make for the gospel being belied by our actions.
By your grace, refashion us deep within,
and make us more completely the people you would have us be.
Put a new heart and a right spirit within us,
so that everything we say, do and are may truly speak of you.
Amen.

A woman's place? The blight of sexism

Opening prayer

Living God,
thank you for making us different,
man and woman,
each having particular gifts,
particular characteristics,
particular instincts,
particular qualities.
But thank you also that, overriding everything that sets us apart,
we are bound by a common humanity,
male and female having as much to contribute,
as much right to lead,
as much potential as the other.
Teach us today more of what that means,
and help us to recognise some of the injustices women have faced
across the centuries,
including those that continue to this day.
Help us, within the Church,
to allow for the views of those who think differently than we do,
but also to do all that we can to put right what we consider to
be wrongs,
so that the legacy we leave to those who come after us may be
one that both they,
and we,
can truly be proud of.
Amen.

Key passage

For in Christ Jesus you are all children of God through faith. As
many of you as were baptised into Christ have clothed yourselves
with Christ. There is no longer Jew or Greek, there is no longer

slave or free, there is no longer male and female; for all of you are one in Christ Jesus. And if you belong to Christ, then you are Abraham's offspring, heirs according to the promise.

Galatians 3:26-29

Ice-breaker

Invite participants to pair off and play a variant game of draughts together – see the site http://www.di.fc.ul.pt/~jpn/gv/checkers.htm for details of variants (e.g. Canadian Checkers, German Checkers, Italian Checkers, Russian Checkers, Spanish Checkers, Thai Checkers, Turkish Checkers etc.) and how to play them. (You will need to prepare for this before the session, ensuring you have sufficient sets of draughts and boards to accommodate everyone. You will also need to succinctly explain the rules of the variation.) Set a time limit to ensure that this ice-breaker does not take over the session.

Introduction

Every woman should be filled with shame by the thought that she is a woman . . . the consciousness of their own nature must evoke feelings of shame. (Clement of Alexandria: *c.* 150–215; theologian and Church Father)

Men should not sit and listen to a woman . . . even if she says admirable things, or even saintly things, that is of little consequence, since it came from the mouth of a woman. (Origen: *c.* 185–232; theologian and Church Father)

And do you not know that you are (each) an Eve? The sentence of God on this sex of yours lives in this age: the guilt must of necessity live too. You are the devil's gateway: you are the unsealer of that (forbidden) tree: you are the first deserter of the divine law: you are she who persuaded him whom the devil was not valiant enough to attack. You destroyed so easily God's image, man. On account of your desert – that is, death – even the Son of God had to die. And do you think about adorning yourself over and above your tunics of skins? (Tertullian: *c.* 160–225; Church Father)

God maintained the order of each sex by dividing the business of life into two parts, and assigned the more necessary and beneficial aspects to the man and the less important, inferior matter to the woman. (Chrysostom: *c.* 347–407; Archbishop of Constantinople and Doctor of the Church)

Woman is the root of all evil. (Jerome: *c.* 347–420; priest, theologian, Doctor of the Church and Church Father)

I don't see what sort of help woman was created to provide man with, if one excludes procreation. If woman is not given to man for help in bearing children, for what help could she be? To till the earth together? If help were needed for that, man would have been a better help for man. The same goes for comfort in solitude. How much more pleasure is it for life and conversation when two friends live together than when a man and a woman cohabitate? . . . the woman together with her own husband is the image of God, so that that whole substance may be one image; but when she is referred separately to her quality of help-meet, which regards the woman herself alone, then she is not the image of God; but as regards the man alone, he is the image of God as fully and completely as when the woman too is joined with him in one. (Augustine: 354–430; Bishop of Hippo, Doctor of the Church and Church Father)

The woman certainly differs from the man, for she is weaker in body and intellect. Nevertheless Eve was an excellent creature and equal to Adam in so far as the divine image: that is, righteousness, wisdom and eternal salvation, is concerned. Still, she was only a woman. As the sun is much more glorious than the moon (though also the moon is glorious), so the woman was inferior to the man both in honour and dignity, though she, too, was a very excellent work of God. (Martin Luther: 1483–1546; German priest, theologian and Protestant Reformer)

Of the first post-resurrection appearance of Jesus to women rather than to men: 'I consider this was done by way of reproach, because they [the men] had been so tardy and sluggish to believe. And indeed, they deserve not only to have *women* for their teachers, but even oxen and asses . . . Yet it pleased the Lord, by means of those weak and contemptible vessels, to give display of his power.' (John Calvin: 1509–64; French theologian, pastor and Protestant Reformer)

[Women are] weake, fraile, impatient, feeble and foolish. (John Knox: *c.* 1514–72; Scottish clergyman and Protestant Reformer)

Do you squirm with embarrassment and shame when you read words like those above? *I* do. They illustrate with shocking clarity the blinkered and rampant sexism that has all too often blighted the history of the Church, and I for one feel disgusted to be part of an institution that has come out with such statements and perpetuated such views. It would help, of course, if we could safely claim that ideas such as the above have been irrevocably confined to history. But have they? Long-running debates in the Church of England over women priests and bishops would suggest not, and non-conformist Churches cannot sit back complacently, for though women clergy had theoretically long been accepted among their ranks, the reality is that they are still frequently discriminated against, finding it hard to secure a position. All this despite the fact that women are the mainstay of most congregations, making up the majority of the congregation and frequently taking on a greater share of their church's work and responsibilities. It would be quite wrong to suggest that sexism as such is generally endemic among Christians, for in most cases nothing could be further from the truth, but vestiges of it within the Church nonetheless live on today. In this session we will examine the roots and manifestations of this further, specifically in relation to the issue of women clergy and bishops.

Bible verses

What the Bible has to say about women and their place in the Church doesn't always make pleasant reading. There seems to be no getting away from the fact that the attitude frequently conveyed is sexist at best, if not downright misogynistic. Witness, for example, the following verses; though – as we shall see in the subsequent study section – they do not tell the whole of the biblical story:

1 Corinthians 11:5

Any woman who prays or prophesies with her head unveiled disgraces her head – it is one and the same thing as having her head shaved.

1 Corinthians 14:34, 35

Women should be silent in the churches. For they are not permitted to speak, but should be subordinate, as the law also says. If there is anything they desire to know, let them ask their husbands at home. For it is shameful for a woman to speak in church.

Ephesians 5:23, 24

For the husband is the head of the wife just as Christ is the head of the church, the body of which he is the Saviour. Just as the church is subject to Christ, so also wives ought to be, in everything, to their husbands.

1 Timothy 2:11-15

Let a woman learn in silence with full submission. I permit no woman to teach or to have authority over a man; she is to keep silent. For Adam was formed first, then Eve; and Adam was not deceived, but the woman was deceived and became a transgressor. Yet she will be saved through childbearing, provided they continue in faith and love and holiness, with modesty.

Titus 2:3-5

Likewise, tell the older women to be reverent in behaviour, not to be slanderers or slaves to drink; they are to teach what is good, so that they may encourage the young women to love their husbands, to love their children, to be self-controlled, chaste, good managers of the household, kind, being submissive to their husbands, so that the word of God may not be discredited.

1 Peter 3:1-5

Wives, in the same way, accept the authority of your husbands, so that, even if some of them do not obey the word, they may be won over without a word by their wives' conduct, when they see the purity and reverence of your lives. Do not adorn yourselves outwardly by braiding your hair, and by wearing gold ornaments or fine clothing; rather, let your adornment be the inner self with the lasting beauty of a gentle and quiet spirit, which is very precious in God's sight. It was in this way long ago that the holy women who hoped in God used to adorn themselves by accepting the authority of their husbands.

Study

On the basis of the above, is there any getting away from the fact that the Bible, and hence Christianity itself, is inherently sexist? Well, yes and no. If we take up a literalist stance in relation to Scripture, then we've got a problem, for there's no explaining away the implications of these verses. Surely, though, we need to remember that passages such as these were written in centuries when patriarchal dominance was the norm and largely unquestioned, as seen from the quotes of Church Fathers given in the introduction to this session. That doesn't justify the sentiments for a moment, but it does help to explain them, and perhaps what should surprise us is not that we so often encounter chauvinism in the pages of Scripture but that we also frequently encounter a respect for and appreciation of the role of women that was remarkably progressive for its time.

In the Old Testament, we read of Miriam, the prophetess (Exodus 15:20), Deborah the prophetess (Judges 4:4, 5), and Huldah the prophetess (2 Kings 22:14), and women such as Esther, Naomi, Ruth are held up as examples of faith, to be revered and respected. Likewise, in the New Testament, Anna is described as a prophetess in Luke 2:36, while Dorcas (Acts 9:36-42) is celebrated for her Christian devotion and charity. Besides the apostles, numerous women followed Jesus throughout his ministry (including Mary Magdalene, Susanna, Joanna and Salome, not to mention his devoted friends, Martha and Mary), some of these staying more faithful to him at the time of his crucifixion than many of the disciples, who fled for their lives. Even the Apostle Paul, regarded by many as being the quintessential chauvinist, frequently commends the contribution of women to the life and witness of the Church. In Romans, for example, he refers to Phoebe, a servant of the church at Cenchreae (16:1) who should be treated in a way 'fitting for the saints'; to Prisca (elsewhere called Priscilla), a 'fellow worker' in Christ; to 'Mary, who has worked hard for you' (16:6), to Junia, 'prominent among the apostles' (16:7), and to Tryphaena, Tryphosa and Persis, who have 'worked hard in the Lord' (16:12). In 2 Timothy 1:5 he applauds the faith of Timothy's mother, Eunice, and grandmother, Lois; in Philippians 4:2, 3 he pays tribute to Eoudia and Syntyche, who 'struggled beside me in the work of the gospel'; while in Acts 16 he preaches to Lydia who goes on to found a church in her own home.

The message of the Bible, then, is thankfully not as unequivocally sexist as it might first appear. So how do we account for the near-misogyny it has sometimes been used to justify? Discrimination against, and even hatred of, women, goes back to the story of Adam and Eve, in which Eve is cast as the root of all mankind's problems through her leading astray of Adam. As a result, women in general were subsequently regarded as morally and intellectually inferior, not to mention as temptresses intent on luring men away from God. Drawing such a conclusion is the height of folly, illustrating once again the danger of insisting on a literal interpretation of the Bible. Had a *woman* been allowed to write the account (which, of course, she wouldn't have been!) , it could just as well have portrayed Adam as the tempter, and would probably also have featured Eve created first with Adam subsequently fashioned from a rib taken from *her* body!

The Genesis Adam and Eve story, and much of the attitude towards women in religious circles subsequently, probably owes much, as Katharine M. Rogers has observed in her book, *The Troublesome Helpmate*, to male hang-ups about sex and fear of female seduction. Sigmund Freud, for all of the weaknesses of his some of his arguments, was almost certainly right that various aspects of the monotheistic world religions owe much to men's guilt concerning their own sexual urges and inability to control them. Whereas Western society in general has frequently objectivised women as sexual playthings, religion has excluded them from temple and synagogue, hidden them beneath burkas, or denied them a role within leadership roles, thus effectively keeping them firmly at arm's length. In each instance, women are made to pay for men's lusts and insecurities – a fact reflected, it's hard not to feel, in at least some of the Apostle Paul's pronouncements on the role and status of women within the Church, as well as in the Church's general attitude towards women subsequently.

The perception of women within the Church has also unquestionably been shaped by, and helped to shape, a patriarchal view of society that, until recent times, had gone largely unchallenged. Men were the top dogs, the providers, those in authority – women should stick to their place in the kitchen or nursery: that, essentially, was the way of things for the bulk of human history. In marital relationships, men expected to be the dominant party and for their wives to be submissive; a fact once again reflected in Paul's writings, as we have seen.

Yet, as our key verse – also written by Paul – reminds us (Galatians 3:28), 'there is no longer male and female; for all of you are one in Christ Jesus'. Push this to its logical conclusion and we have the basis for what is frequently implied in Paul's commendation of women within his letters: an equal place for both female and male as mutual partners in the life and ministry of the Church.

It seems unfair to single out the Anglican Church as an example of where female ministry continues to be a bone of contention, for Roman Catholicism has thus far refused point blank even to countenance the possibility of either women priests or bishops (let alone the idea of a female pope!), and non-conformists are by no means always as enlightened as their official practices might suggest, some hard-line traditionalists effectively elevating chauvinism to a sacred virtue – but it is in the Church of England that the role of ministry has most publicly been a hot potato in recent years. Credit should go to it for the way it has addressed and continues to address the issue; progress may have been painfully slow, but it has been made nonetheless.

Before 1992 there were no official women priests in the Church of England, but following their authorisation in that year they were first ordained in 1994. Subsequently, according to a *Guardian* report of 11 February 2014: between 2002 and 2012, the number of female full-time clergy has increased by 41 per cent from 1,262 to 1,781, while 'the number of full-time males has dropped from 7,920 to 6,017, meaning women now make up roughly one in five members of full-time clergy (but only one in seven of those in incumbent posts such as vicars and priests-in-charge). Just under half of part-time clergy are women and over half of the 3,148 ministers who support themselves are [women] too.' However, 'there are only 39 female senior members of the clergy compared to 319 males'. Clearly, then, the ministry of women is increasingly being valued by many, and without their participation the Anglican Church in this country would probably struggle to function in its present form. Yet, sadly, a significant number of churches are still fundamentally opposed to women priests and refuse to accept them, insisting for ultimate pastoral oversight on so-called flying bishops (technically, Provisional Episcopal

Visitors) as those 'untainted' by any participation in women's ordination.

If the battle for women priests is still not wholly won, that for women bishops – at the time of writing at least – is still less so. The last General Synod vote on the issue took place in November 2012 when, perhaps due to a late amendment, the bill was defeated by a mere six votes in the House of Laity, despite having been passed in the House of Bishops and House of Clergy, the result reducing Rowan Williams, then Archbishop of Canterbury, to tears. Newspaper headlines and leader articles summed up the general public view of the decision, which was, as Rowan Williams had feared, that the Church had lost its credibility. As the *Independent* put it:

To the secular world, the case for women to become bishops is the same as that regarding the priesthood. It is a matter of equality and inclusion. In fairness, most people inside the Church agree, seeing inclusion and equality before God as central values of the Christian gospel.

The majority of bishops, priests and lay members of the Church have long accepted that. But, because of the highly cautious structures of the established Church, a two-thirds majority was needed in all three houses of its General Synod to effect change.

And that has allowed a recalcitrant minority to prevent the Church from entering the 20th, let alone the 21st, century.

The Times was equally damning:

What happened yesterday will be horribly familiar to leaders of political parties that have lost their way. The process was hijacked by a small but highly motivated group of fundamentalists more interested in factional organisation, textual analysis and strict orthodoxy than in the real world and how people live their lives.

When such people take over any body it drifts away from common sense.

The *Daily Mail* was slightly more cautious, but noted:

> Yes, we respect the theological objections of those in the House of Laity who, by the narrowest of margins, denied supporters of the move the two-thirds majority they needed.
>
> But the vote has condemned the Church to years more infighting over a question which most of the nation finds abstruse or simply bewildering.
>
> It also highlights a worrying divide between churchgoers and the clergy, who overwhelmingly supported promoting women . . .

Moves to fast-track legislation that could see the first woman bishops appointed by late 2014 are due to be voted on shortly, so some may be in place as you read this book. Time will tell, but opposition to women bishops among some evangelicals, Anglo-Catholics and traditionalists within the Church of England remains strong and frequently bitter.

In some countries, member Churches of the Anglican Communion have pressed on with appointing women bishops regardless – notably, the Episcopal Church in the United States; the Church of Ireland; the Anglican Churches of Aotearoa, New Zealand, and Polynesia; the Anglican Church of Australia; the Anglican Church of Canada; the Church of Southern Africa; the Church of South India; and the Episcopal Church of Cuba – and the Church in Wales is well on its way to doing the same. In other countries, however, particularly in Africa and Latin America, Churches of the Anglican Communion remain implacably opposed to the idea of women bishops, to the point of threatening schism should the go-ahead be given for it.

It would be wrong, of course, to accuse all opponents of women's ordination of outright sexism. Many would claim to be following their conscience, standing up for what they believe to be in accordance with biblical teaching, and however much we may disagree with their interpretation we cannot simply force our opinion upon them. Yet we must not forget either that, for generations, women were denied – and some are still denied – an equal place in the ministry of the Church. Can that possibly be right?

Discussion

- Opponents of women bishops, and indeed women priests, will say that the twelve apostles of Jesus were all male, showing that he envisaged an all-male leadership of the Church? Is this a valid argument? If not, why not?
- Does it matter what the world thinks of the Church? Do you think the controversies over women priests and bishops, and the Anglican Church's unwillingness to ordain these, has cost the Church credibility in the eyes of the world? Are women truly given an equal place in the leadership of other denominations?
- Does the Church need to move with the times? What are the dangers of applying this as a general argument? What are the dangers of not doing so? Is the Church sometimes put to shame by the progressive insights of secular society? Does faith sometimes blind people to the need for change?
- How far has principle been used as a mask for prejudice in the debate over women priests and bishops? Do you think sexism still has a hold within the Church? How far, and in what areas, does that extend?
- What do you make of the New Testament passages quoted above concerning the place and role of women within the Church and society? How would you answer some of the apparently sexist implications of what they say? What do you make of the other biblical passages and examples cited?
- Given Paul's words to the Galatians about there no longer being any male or female, but all of us being one in Christ, how do you explain the fact that the Church is struggling to keep up with overcoming discrimination against women, rather than giving a lead?
- Do you see the provision of alternative episcopal oversight in the Church of England, for those who disagree with women

priests, as a way of fudging the issue, designed to hold together the Anglican Communion at all costs, or is it an essential compromise in respecting the convictions of others? Could the Church fail to provide this and at the same time avoid foisting an opinion upon others?

Quotes

Reflect individually on the following quotations for a moment, then discuss together which, if any, people found most helpful. What point is each making? What lessons can be learned from them? What challenge do they make to us, personally, and to the Church in general.

- You don't have to be anti-man to be pro-woman. (Jane Galvin Lewis)
- Women are the only exploited group in history to have been idealised into powerlessness. (Erica Jong)
- Humankind is made up of two sexes, women and men. Is it possible for humankind to grow by the improvement of only one part while the other part is ignored? Is it possible that if half of a mass is tied to earth with chains that the other half can soar into skies? (Mustafa Kemal Atatürk)
- Feminism is the radical notion that women are people. (Cheris Kramarae and Paula Treichler)
- Of all the evils for which man has made himself responsible, none is so degrading, so shocking or so brutal as his abuse of the better half of humanity; the female sex. (Mahatma Gandhi)
- Remember, all men would be tyrants if they could. If particular care and attention is not paid to the ladies we are determined to foment a rebellion, and will not hold ourselves bound by any laws in which we have no voice, or representation. (Abigail Adams)
- I think, therefore I'm single. (Lizz Winstead)
- Men are taught to apologise for their weaknesses, women for their strengths. (Lois Wyse)

- Because I am a woman, I must make unusual efforts to succeed. If I fail, no one will say, 'She doesn't have what it takes.' They will say, 'Women don't have what it takes.' (Clare Boothe Luce)
- Woman is the companion of man, gifted with equal mental capacity. (Mahatma Gandhi)
- Every time we liberate a woman, we liberate a man. (Margaret Mead)
- No nation can ever be worthy of its existence that cannot take its women along with the men. No struggle can ever succeed without women participating side by side with men. There are two powers in the world; one is the sword and the other is the pen. There is a great competition and rivalry between the two. There is a third power stronger than both, that of the women. (Muhammad Ali Jinnah)
- I believe that it is as much a right and duty for women to do something with their lives as for men and we are not going to be satisfied with such frivolous parts as you give us. (Louisa May Alcott)
- Women are the only oppressed group in our society that lives in intimate association with their oppressors. (Evelyn Cunningham)
- Sure God created man before woman. But then you always make a rough draft before the final masterpiece. (Unknown)
- The test of whether or not you can hold a job should not be in the arrangement of your chromosomes. (Bella Abzug)
- Women who seek to be equal with men lack ambition. (Timothy Leary/Marilyn Monroe)
- A man has every season while a woman only has the right to spring. (Jane Fonda)
- Women's chains have been forged by men, not by anatomy. (Estelle R. Ramey)
- Whether women are better than men I cannot say – but I can say they are certainly no worse. (Golda Meir)
- It starts when you sink in his arms and ends with your arms in his sink. (Unknown)

Final thoughts

Less than a hundred years ago, at the time of writing, women in the UK were still ineligible to vote, it not being until 1928 that all women were given the same voting rights as men. That's an incredible thought, isn't it, yet it speaks volumes about the way women have been regarded and treated across the centuries. Militant feminism in its extremist forms may have its detractors, but there can be no doubt that the feminist movement in general has been vital, and has done much to put right flagrant wrongs that were integral to our society until all too recently. Many of these, indeed, continue to this day, women still being overlooked for high positions in numerous walks of life, despite being eminently qualified; still frequently being paid less for doing the same job; and still often being confronted by a host of sexist attitudes and preconceptions. What signal has the Church given to the world through its own attitude towards and treatment of women? Has it helped to challenge the scourge of sexism, or does it still unconsciously perpetuate it?

Closing prayer

Loving God,
thank you for creating humankind in your image,
male and female.
Thank you for making us one in Christ,
each having an equal share in the work of your kingdom.
Thank you for the immeasurable contribution women have made
across the years,
in countless ways,
to the life of the world and of your people –
for the gifts they have brought to bear,
the sacrifices they have made,
the vision, dedication and perseverance they have shown.
Forgive the ways women have all too often been
discriminated against,
marginalised not only in society
but also in in the life of the Church,

their talents undervalued,
their creativity stifled,
their contribution overlooked,
their rights ignored.
Defend the cause of women everywhere,
and prosper those who work in positions of authority
and responsibility,
both outside and within the Church.
Amen.

Straight talking: the blight of homophobia

Opening prayer

Loving God,
we find it hard when our moral parameters are questioned,
when opinions we've been taught from childhood are challenged
and long-held convictions are undermined.
Yet we know that sometimes we need the courage to think again,
to revise our beliefs,
even to change our point of view completely.
Give us the courage to do that, where necessary,
especially when our views potentially impinge upon the welfare
of others.
Save us from clinging rigidly to ideas without thinking them
through;
from being so sure of our rightness that we refuse to countenance
any other possibility.
Forgive the chequered legacy we inherit as your Church,
and give us wisdom, love and humility in all our dealings
with others,
so that we may leave a better heritage behind us,
through Jesus Christ our Lord.
Amen.

Key passage

'Do not judge, so that you may not be judged. For with the
judgement you make you will be judged, and the measure you
give will be the measure you get. Why do you see the speck in
your neighbour's eye, but do not notice the log in your own eye?
Or how can you say to your neighbour, "Let me take the speck out
of your eye", while the log is in your own eye? You hypocrite, first
take the log out of your own eye, and then you will see clearly to
take the speck out of your neighbour's eye.'   *Matthew 7:1-5*

51

Ice-breaker

Invite participants to pair off and play a variant game of draughts together – see the site http://www.di.fc.ul.pt/~jpn/gv/checkers.htm for details of variants (e.g. Canadian Checkers, German Checkers, Italian Checkers, Russian Checkers, Spanish Checkers, Thai Checkers, Turkish Checkers etc.) and how to play them. (You will need to prepare for this before the session, ensuring you have sufficient sets of draughts and boards to accommodate everyone. You will also need to succinctly explain the rules of the variation.) Set a time limit to ensure that this ice-breaker does not take over the session.

Introduction

In April 1895, the celebrated author, Oscar Wilde, was arrested in London charged with 'gross indecency' – a euphemism for homosexual acts – and put on trial. Found guilty a month later, he was sentenced to two years' hard labour, which he undertook first from Pentonville and subsequently from Wandsworth prison. Such were the conditions and treatment he endured there that in November he collapsed from illness and hunger, rupturing his right ear drum in the process – an injury that was possibly linked to the meningitis from which he died five years later. Pilloried and reviled on account of his homosexuality, he spent the rest of his life 'exiled' in Europe, his reputation in tatters.

In 1952, Alan Turing – probably one of the most brilliant minds Britain has ever produced and a man whose work at Bletchley Park during the Second World War contributed immeasurably to the Allies' final victory – was prosecuted for homosexuality, still deemed a criminal offence in the UK at the time (indeed, it remained so until the Sexual Offences Act of 1967). Turing was given a choice between imprisonment and 'treatment' with female hormones to 'cure' his homosexuality. He chose the latter, a course of 'therapy' that not only rendered him impotent but led to a condition known as gynecomastia – effectively, the growth of breasts. He died two years later, just short of his forty-second birthday, as a result of cyanide poisoning – most probably taken intentionally.

In 1998 the talented English footballer, Justin Fashanu – who, among other clubs, played for Norwich City, West Bromwich Albion, Nottingham Forest and Southampton – was found hanged in a lockup garage in London, having committed suicide following allegations made against him of sexual assault. The first, and so far only professional footballer to public acknowledge his homosexuality while still playing the game, he was so convinced he had no chance of a fair trial that he took his own life.

So we could go on . . . and on . . . and on. History is littered with the stories of men and women who have been persecuted, driven to despair, pushed to the point of suicide, on account of their sexuality. They have been lampooned as 'poofs', 'fairies', 'nancy boys', 'dykes', and a whole lot worse; ostracised and hounded as perverts and deviants, to be viewed with suspicion, fear, pity or hatred.

Happily, attitudes have changed beyond recognition over the past quarter of a century. Most people, particularly the younger generation, are far more accepting of differing expressions of sexuality that those in generations past. But what of the Church? There too, if truth be told, many are more open than was once the case, but typically such openness is acknowledged only in private, almost whispered as a guilty secret. Official pronouncements, meanwhile, tend to be more reactionary, it still being common to hear homosexuality condemned as a sin, contrary to the will and purpose of God and to the laws of nature. Admittedly, the Church of England asserted as far back as 1991 – in a statement by the House of Bishops titled *Issues in Human Sexuality* – that same-sex partnerships are acceptable for laypersons, if not for gay clergy, but a vociferous and influential wing within the Anglican Communion, and many other evangelical and conservative Christians, have continued to campaign long and hard against gay relationships in any shape or form. So, on what is the Church's traditional antipathy to homosexuality based? Let's look at the key biblical verses usually cited.

Bible verses

Genesis 19:1-11

The two angels came to Sodom in the evening, and Lot was sitting in the gateway of Sodom. When Lot saw them, he rose to meet them, and bowed down with his face to the ground. He said, 'Please, my lords, turn aside to your servant's house and spend the night, and wash your feet; then you can rise early and go on your way.' They said, 'No; we will spend the night in the square.' But he urged them strongly; so they turned aside to him and entered his house; and he made them a feast, and baked unleavened bread, and they ate.

But before they lay down, the men of the city, the men of Sodom, both young and old, all the people to the last man, surrounded the house; and they called to Lot, 'Where are the men who came to you tonight? Bring them out to us, so that we may know them.' Lot went out of the door to the men, shut the door after him, and said, 'I beg you, my brothers, do not act so wickedly. Look, I have two daughters who have not known a man; let me bring them out to you, and do to them as you please; only do nothing to these men, for they have come under the shelter of my roof.' But they replied, 'Stand back!' And they said, 'This fellow came here as an alien, and he would play the judge! Now we will deal worse with you than with them.' Then they pressed hard against the man Lot, and came near the door to break it down. But the men inside reached out their hands and brought Lot into the house with them, and shut the door. And they struck with blindness the men who were at the door of the house, both small and great, so that they were unable to find the door.

Judges 19:22-25a

While they were enjoying themselves, the men of the city, a perverse lot, surrounded the house, and started pounding on the door. They said to the old man, the master of the house, 'Bring out the man who came into your house, so that we may have intercourse with him.' And the man, the master of the house, went out to them and said to them, 'No, my brothers, do not act so wickedly. Since this man is my guest, do not do this vile thing. Here are my virgin daughter and his concubine; let me bring them out now. Ravish them and do whatever you want to them; but against this man do not do such a vile thing.' But the men would not listen to him. So the man seized his concubine, and put her out to them. They wantonly raped her, and abused her all through the night until the morning.

Leviticus 18:22

You shall not lie with a male as with a woman; it is an abomination.

Leviticus 20:13

If a man lies with a male as with a woman, both of them have committed an abomination; they shall be put to death; their blood is upon them.

Romans 1:26, 27

For this reason God gave them up to degrading passions. Their women exchanged natural intercourse for unnatural, and in the same way also the men, giving up natural intercourse with women, were consumed with passion for one another. Men committed shameless acts with men and received in their own persons the due penalty for their error.

1 Corinthians 6:9

Do you not know that wrongdoers will not inherit the kingdom of God? Do not be deceived! Fornicators, idolaters, adulterers, male prostitutes, sodomites . . .

1 Timothy 1:9-10

This means understanding that the law is laid down not for the innocent but for the lawless and disobedient, for the godless and sinful, for the unholy and profane, for those who kill their father or mother, for murderers, fornicators, sodomites, slave traders, liars, perjurers, and whatever else is contrary to the sound teaching . . .

Study and discussion

What do we make of the above passages? When we look at them carefully, their message is ambiguous:

- Traditionally, the destruction of Sodom and Gomorrah has been put down to its people's penchant for homosexuality, yet what actually seems to be condemned here is not homosexual practice, as such, but the attempted gang rape of guests, as in the similar story found in Judges 19. In Genesis, the situation is complicated by the guests being identified as 'angels', it being their divine nature that makes their attempted rape all the more shocking. According to Ezekiel 16:49: 'the guilt of your sister Sodom [was that] she and her daughters had pride, excess of food, and prosperous ease, but did not aid the poor and needy'. What do you make of this interpretation?

- The verses from Leviticus are probably those most frequently quoted relating to homosexuality in the whole Bible, yet they comprise the merest fraction of a long list or rules and regulations associated with the Jewish law, almost all of which Christians completely ignore. There are decrees, for example, concerning menstruation, haircuts, animal sacrifices, hygiene, tattoos, and so forth; even against wearing clothes made of mixed fabric or eating shellfish! How can anyone justify treating these as irrelevant yet cling rigidly to a few verses on homosexuality?

- The concern of the Apostle Paul in Romans 1 was almost certainly with those who practised fertility rites involving homosexual orgies with temple prostitutes. As a man of his time, he most likely was anti-gay, but his condemnation here relates to a very specific situation rather than to homosexuality per se. How important do you think the context is here for understanding Paul's words?

- Again, the Greek word *malokois* in 1 Corinthians 6:9, and *arsenokoitai* used both there and in 1 Timothy 1.10, literally mean 'soft' and probably refer once more to effeminate male prostitutes and those paying for sex with them. In other words, the sin being condemned is the hiring of someone for sex, not being homosexual oneself.

- Biblical censure of a man lying with another man, as if with a woman, reflects a general view in the ancient world that this was demeaning for one specific reason: that it involved a man taking a passive rather than dominant sexual role. In other words, the condemnation stemmed from sexist and, ultimately, patriarchal attitudes towards women and the sexual act. Can this really be the basis for a balanced appraisal of homosexuality?

- Through condemning homosexuality as a sin, and driving it underground, has the Church been at least partly responsible for creating a culture of licentiousness among some homosexuals rather than one of long-term committed and loving relationships?

- The celebrated South African archbishop, Desmond Tutu, commenting on the issue of homosexuality just days after the election of the openly gay Gene Robinson as a bishop in the US Episcopal Church on 5 August 2003, declared, 'In our Church here in South Africa, that doesn't make a difference. We just say that at the moment, we believe that they should remain celibate and we don't see what the fuss is about.' He has criticised the Church for spending time disagreeing on sexual orientation 'when we face so many devastating problems – poverty, HIV/AIDS, war and conflict'. Do you think the Church has its priorities right or has focused too much on the question of homosexuality at the cost of other, more important issues?

- The list of those known or reputed to be gay includes Alexander the Great, Socrates, Richard the Lionheart, Saladin, Erasmus, Michelangelo, Leonardo da Vinci, Francis Bacon, Queen Anne, Lord Byron, Hans Christian Andersen, Gertrude Stein, Virginia Woolf, Leonard Bernstein, T.E. Lawrence, Tennessee Williams, J.M. Keynes, Ludwig Wittgenstein, Noel Coward, Rock Hudson and Rudolf Nureyev, among countless others. What sort of prejudice and obstacles must these people have had to face in their own particular time and circumstances?

- The Genesis and Judges passages above condemn homosexuality (at least according to their traditional interpretation) but seem to see nothing wrong in consigning young girls to be raped in order to prevent this. What does this say about the biblical worldview, and about these verses' credibility in terms of making moral judgements on the basis of them?

Quotes

Reflect individually on the following quotations for a moment, then discuss together which, if any, people found most helpful. What point is each making? What lessons can be learned from them? What challenge do they make to us, personally, and to the Church in general.

- What's unnatural is homophobia. Homo sapiens is the only species in all of nature that responds with hate to homosexuality. (Alex Sanchez)
- The whole world goes on and on about love. Poets spend their lives writing about it. Everyone thinks it's the most wonderful thing. But, when you mention two guys in love, they forget all that and freak out. (Mark A. Roeder)
- The only thing wrong with being gay is how some people treat you when they find out. (Robin Reardon)
- To be raped is to be sexually violated. For society to force someone, through shame and ostracism, to comply with love and sex that it defines, is nothing but organised rape. That is what homophobia is all about. Organised rape. (Lee Maracle)
- Social conservatives seem to see a bigger threat to marriage from committed gay couples who want in on it than from straight ones who opt out of it. (Margaret Talbot)
- Homophobia is like racism and anti-Semitism and other forms of bigotry in that it seeks to dehumanise a large group of people, to deny their humanity, their dignity and personhood. This sets the stage for further repression and violence that spread all too easily to victimise the next minority group. (Coretta Scott King)
- The sad truth about bigotry is that most bigots either don't realise that they are bigots, or they convince themselves that their bigotry is perfectly justified. (Wayne Gerard Trotman)

Final thoughts

Like most of my generation, I was brought up to see homosexuality as something odd; and, as a heterosexual male, I still struggle to get my head round the idea of two men finding each other sexually attractive; but neither of those facts could justify me in claiming that homosexuality is wrong. Each has more to do with personal prejudice than with anything else. Yet that takes us to the root of this issue, for it is prejudice, I suspect, that lies behind the pronouncements and actions of most opponents of gay rights, however much those might be cloaked by appeals to religion. If homosexuality were truly the sin some claim it to be, it is surprising that the Bible has so little to say on the subject, and that its words are open to interpretation. More fundamentally, we must account for why God has made some people gay and others straight, for make no mistake, no one would have chosen to endure the hostility and discrimination that, until recently, has been meted out to homosexuals as a matter of course.

Christians, of all people, should be those least inclined to judge and most accepting of others, yet the Church's preoccupation with sexuality has led it instead to add to gay people's burdens. Sadly, some Christians continue to add to those still further today.

Closing prayer

Father God,
open our eyes to the prejudice that lurks within us,
within society
and within the Church –
prejudice that too easily in the past,
and even still today in the present,
has dismissed as 'perverted',
'sick'
'abnormal'
or 'sinful'
those whose sexuality differs from the 'norm'.
Help us to focus instead on encouraging loving relationships
in which trust and commitment can flourish;
relationships consecrated to you which are able to stand the test
of time.

Forgive the way that so many not considered 'straight' have,
across the years,
endured mockery, suspicion, hostility and persecution,
driving many to the edge of despair
and some of them beyond.
Help us and your people everywhere to be truly welcoming of all,
following together in the footsteps of Christ.
Amen.

Set in stone?
The blight of fundamentalism

Opening prayer

Almighty God,
open our hearts and minds to the ways you speak:
through the Bible,
through prayer,
through the preaching and teaching of your word,
through those around us
and through the wider world.
Save us from limiting what you would say to us by our own
narrow horizons,
however sincere those may be.
Deliver us from a faith that thinks it has all the answers
or that refuses to ask any questions;
a faith that is so concerned with protecting what it sees as truth
that it sets itself up in your place,
resisting anything that may stretch or challenge it?
Help us to study your word with reverence and humility
but also honesty and openness,
so that you may lead us into a deeper understanding of truth,
a fuller grasp of your purpose,
and a deeper experience of who and what you are.
Amen.

Key passage

For my thoughts are not your thoughts, nor are your ways my
ways, says the Lord. For as the heavens are higher than the earth,
so are my ways higher than your ways and my thoughts than
your thoughts.

Isaiah 55:8, 9

Ice-breaker

Invite participants to pair off and play a variant game of draughts together – see the site http://www.di.fc.ul.pt/~jpn/gv/checkers.htm for details of variants (e.g. Canadian Checkers, German Checkers, Italian Checkers, Russian Checkers, Spanish Checkers, Thai Checkers, Turkish Checkers etc.) and how to play them. (You will need to prepare for this before the session, ensuring you have sufficient sets of draughts and boards to accommodate everyone. You will also need to succinctly explain the rules of the variation.) Set a time limit to ensure that this ice-breaker does not take over the session.

Introduction

It was my first term at theological college, a few weeks into my course, when I returned to my room to find a piece of paper that had been pushed under the door. It comprised a list of doctrinal points; points that, in the eyes of the sender, people must believe in order to be considered a Christian. And the implication – summed up in a challenge written in large bold capital letters at the bottom of the page: 'BROTHER, ARE YOU SAVED!!?' – was clearly that I fell short of the mark. In the eyes of at least one individual, my faith was evidently suspect, my beliefs less than sound.

Was I alone in receiving such a missive? Sadly not. I soon discovered that any student open to theological scholarship and rational criticism of the Bible was likely to receive the same treatment, swiftly becoming tainted with the dread charge of 'liberalism', shorthand in the eyes of a certain group for 'heresy'. Through my willingness to employ the same tools of reason applied in all other fields of human enquiry I had automatically failed their criteria for being considered a Bible-believing Christian, and was consequently taboo.

There's nothing new in such an attitude, nor is it by any means a thing of the past. There have always been – and probably always will be – those eager to insist that their understanding of the Bible, and of faith itself, is the *only* right one. Never mind the fact that, as we have seen in earlier sessions, there is much in Scripture's pages that even the most hard-line of Christians in fact ignores. Never mind that – as well as several other genres – it comprises a mixture of legend, history, poetry, letters and prophecy, each written for a different purpose in contrasting circumstances. Never mind that it contains inconsistences and ambiguities that need to be wrestled with and accounted for. Never mind that it was written in Greek and Hebrew, and that much in its pages is not only difficult to translate accurately but is also inevitably open to interpretation. The Bible, some insist, is the literal and inerrant word of God that must be accepted as it stands and cannot be questioned in any way. Thus, for example, many schools in the Bible Belt of the American Midwest refuse to teach anything about evolution; instead, they espouse creationism – the idea that God created the universe in seven days, exactly as stated in the book of Genesis – and they teach this as the one and only truth. The evidence of geology, and of science in general, is simply dismissed as irrelevant.

So what claims does the Bible actually make for itself? The answer, surprisingly, is very few, as we will see below.

Bible verses

Certain verses speak of the importance of Scripture for building up our faith and so forth, but none claims that everything in its pages is the literal word of God (words of Paul to Timothy perhaps come closest to this, though the Scripture he refers to would have been the Old Testament – the New Testament not having been compiled at the time – and the claim he actually makes for it is much more modest). Indeed, other verses remind us that God is beyond our understanding, greater than we can ever begin to comprehend, which surely counsels us against limiting his will or way to any one interpretation of Scripture, literal or otherwise. All the books of the Bible were written at a specific time, in a specific place for a specific purpose, and they were inevitably coloured by that in all kinds of ways, meaning that when we read them we need sometimes to separate the wheat from the chaff, the husk from the kernel, if God is truly to speak.

Reflect quietly upon the following passages before moving on to study and discussion.

Psalm 119:105
Your word is a lamp to my feet and a light to my path.

Ecclesiastes 5:2
Never be rash with your mouth, nor let your heart be quick to utter a word before God, for God is in heaven, and you upon earth; therefore let your words be few.

Romans 15:4
For whatever was written in former days was written for our instruction, so that by steadfastness and by the encouragement of the scriptures we might have hope.

2 Timothy 3:16, 17
All scripture is inspired by God and is useful for teaching, for reproof, for correction, and for training in righteousness, so that everyone who belongs to God may be proficient, equipped for every good work.

Hebrews 4:12
Indeed, the word of God is living and active, sharper than any two-edged sword, piercing until it divides soul from spirit, joints from marrow; it is able to judge the thoughts and intentions of the heart.

Study

So what's wrong with fundamentalism? Isn't it essentially harmless?

In one sense, yes, or at least it would be if it were purely a private affair, but, almost by definition, that isn't the case, for those who are convinced of their rightness inevitably want and expect others to share their convictions. Anyone who fails to do so finds themselves condemned and criticised as a result, and that can have hugely damaging consequences, especially for those who are finding their way in faith.

Equally important, fundamentalism drives many people away from religion, making it seem out of touch and obscurantist, having little in common with the real world. If people today are to take the Bible seriously, let alone base their lives upon it, they require evidence backing up the claims Christians make for it, just as they would expect evidence for any other claims. To argue that Scripture is God's word simply because it says so doesn't hold water (especially given that it doesn't claim this at all!). Different groups make the same claim for their own scriptures and sacred writings; how can we tell which is right and which is wrong?

Furthermore, much in the Bible – particularly the Old Testament – seems to portray a God very different from the loving creator whom Christians claim to worship; a god who apparently quite happily sanctions genocide – including the slaughter of women and children – without so much as a qualm, all of which seems a far cry from the God we claim to see revealed in Christ. Add to this that much of the Bible reflects belief in a three-tiered universe, heaven above, hell below and the earth in between – a cosmology that we know today to be patently false – and the idea that we must accept every word of Scripture as it stands becomes increasingly untenable.

We can't, as Christians, claim exemption from the criteria used by other disciplines to assess and examine truth and falsehood. Nor should we want to. The scholarship of theologians and others who spend their workaday lives studying the Bible and its background does not threaten our faith, as some would suggest, but expands it, opening up new horizons and deeper insights. Yes, it may sometimes pose difficult questions; yes, it may mean rethinking established assumptions and perhaps even reformulating beliefs, but this should be enriching and liberating, yielding fuller understanding. To settle on one particular interpretation of Scripture and close our minds to any other is not only to fall into the trap of bibliolatry – the worship of a book rather than of God himself – but ultimately to set ourselves up in the place of God, as if we have grasped all there is to know and say about him. Yet, as the prophet Isaiah reminds, his thoughts are not our thoughts nor his ways our ways. The language we use of God, our grasp of his purpose let alone of his very nature, will always and inevitably be flawed simply by virtue of who and what he is. As David Tomlinson so eloquently puts it in his deeply perceptive book, *The Bad Christian's Manifesto* (Hodder, 2014), 'The problem arises when we believe that our images and conceptions of God are literally true, that we can actually describe who or what God is. At that point religion turns into idolatry; we replace that which is infinite and indescribable with something finite and ephemeral.' Much the same point was poetically made by the celebrated Christian apologist, C. S. Lewis, in his 'Footnote to all Prayers':

He whom I bow to only knows to whom I bow
When I attempt the ineffable Name, murmuring Thou,
And dream of Pheidian fancies and embrace in heart
Symbols (I know) which cannot be the thing Thou art.
Thus always, taken at their word, all prayers blaspheme
Worshipping with frail images a folk-lore dream,
And all men in their praying, self-deceived, address
The coinage of their own unquiet thoughts, unless
Thou in magnetic mercy to Thyself divert
Our arrows, aimed unskilfully, beyond desert;
And all men are idolaters, crying unheard
To a deaf idol, if Thou take them at their word.
Take not, O Lord, our literal sense. Lord, in thy great
Unbroken speech our limping metaphor translate.

Discussion

- How would you define fundamentalist religion? What causes people to espouse it?
- What experience have you had of fundamentalist Christianity? What are the strengths and weaknesses of the fundamentalist approach?

- What aspects/passages of the Bible do you find it hardest to reconcile with a literal interpretation of Scripture?
- Despite the evidence of the fossil record and the countless other discoveries and insights of geology, and science in general, many creationists insist that the universe was created a mere 6,000 years ago, their calculations being based on the various genealogies of the Bible. How would you respond to such claims? What impression do they give people of the Church? How would you answer them?
- What problems in the Church do you most associate with fundamentalism? What problems has it caused in the world?
- What arguments would you use personally against fundamentalism?

Quotes

Reflect individually on the following quotations for a moment, then discuss together which, if any, people found most helpful. What point is each making? What lessons can be learned from them? What challenge do they make to us, personally, and to the Church in general?

- There are few things more dangerous than inbred religious certainty. (Bart D. Ehrman)
- People wrap themselves in their beliefs. And they do it in such a way that you can't set them free. Not even the truth will set them free. (Michael Specter)
- The man who cannot listen to an argument which opposes his views either has a weak position or is a weak defender of it. No opinion that cannot stand discussion or criticism is worth holding. And it has been wisely said that the man who knows only half of any question is worse off than the man who knows nothing of it. He is not only one sided, but his partisanship soon turns him into an intolerant and a fanatic. In general it is true that nothing which cannot stand up under discussion and criticism is worth defending. (James E. Talmage)
- Without the voice of reason, every faith is its own curse. (Sting)

- In this respect fundamentalism has demonic traits. It destroys the humble honesty of the search for truth, it splits the conscience of its thoughtful adherents, and it makes them fanatical because they are forced to suppress elements of truth of which they are dimly aware. (Paul Tillich)
- It is putting a very high price on one's conjectures to have someone roasted alive on their account. (Michel de Montaigne)
- Anytime that knowledge and a version of the truth are considered to be absolute, fundamentalism is the result, whether the arena is Christianity, Islam, Judaism, or any other religious faith, as well as atheism, conservative or liberal political views, even evolution or intelligent design. Anytime our minds are closed and there is no room for dissent, we are on a slippery slope towards stagnation. (Carlton D. Pearson)
- Philosophy is questions that may never be answered. Religion is answers that may never be questioned. (Unknown)
- The truly wise talk little about religion and are not given to taking sides on doctrinal issues. When they hear people advocating or opposing the claims of this or that party in the church, they turn away with a smile such as men yield to the talk of children. They have no time, they would say, for that kind of thing. They have enough to do in trying to faithfully practise what is beyond dispute. (George MacDonald)
- Of all of the tyrannies that affect mankind, tyranny of religion is the worst. (Thomas Paine)
- Being religious means asking passionately the question of the meaning of our existence and being willing to receive answers, even if the answers hurt. (Paul Tillich)
- Science without religion is lame; religion without science is blind. (Albert Einstein)
- It is unwise to be too sure of one's own wisdom. It is healthy to be reminded that the strongest might weaken and the wisest might err. (Mahatma Gandhi)
- A man must have a good deal of vanity who believes, and a good deal of boldness who affirms, that all the doctrines he holds are true, and all he rejects are false. (Benjamin Franklin)

- Where doubt ends, stupidity begins. (Anon)
- Doubt grows with knowledge. (Johann Wolfgang von Goethe)
- To know much is often the cause of doubting more. (Michel de Montaigne)

Final thoughts

I'm not without sympathy for those who seek refuge in fundamentalism. We live in a rapidly changing world in which nothing can seem stable; a world in which values are constantly changing, today's orthodoxy becoming tomorrow's heresy; a world in which science seems to have all the answers yet leaves us feeling alone in a cold and impersonal universe; a world of moral relativism in which the boundaries between right and wrong are increasingly eroded. How much I've wished sometimes that I could embrace a fundamentalist faith and literal interpretation of Scripture in which everything I'm meant to believe is spelt out for me to the last detail. How much simpler discipleship would be. How much more straightforward the business of being a Christian. But I can no more adopt such a position than I can fly to the moon, for I know that questions of faith are real and the issues confronting the Church are important, demanding of answers. Above all, I know that the errors we've explored in this book – and countless others besides – all stem from an attitude that says I'm right, you're wrong, that insists that truth is set in stone, and that refuses to countenance any other possibility. The irony is that the legacy this leaves is altogether different from the one intended, ultimately denying the very message it aims to protect. Have we sufficient courage and humility to face up to questions of faith, and leave a different legacy instead?

Closing prayer

Gracious God,
forgive us,
for you call us to be your people
shining as light in the world,
yet too often we fail in that calling.

A Chequered Legacy: The Bad and the Ugly

You want our lives to speak of you,
to communicate your grace, mercy, love and acceptance,
yet repeatedly the life of your Church has spoken instead of
human frailty:
of insecurity,
intolerance,
hatred
and selfishness.
Instead of setting free,
religion has been used to bind others;
instead of bringing joy to all,
it has brought misery to many;
instead of building up,
it has torn down.
Faith has been used as a façade to screen prejudice and
preconceptions,
a way of foisting convictions upon others
rather than allowing you to challenge and shape our own.
Have mercy upon us,
and speak now your living word.
Confront what is wrong in our lives,
what is false in our hearts,
and, through your grace, renew us in the likeness of Christ,
so that the legacy we leave behind us may not be a chequered one,
putting across conflicting messages,
but one that speaks unequivocally of you
and of your awesome love for all.
Amen.

Further quotes

Further quotations that you may find useful in stimulating discussion on the themes discussed in this study book can be found at the following websites:

www.notable-quotes.com

www.goodreads.com

www.brainyquote

www.quotegarden.com